W9-BWF-353

DATE DUE

From Egg to Adult
The Life Cycle of Mammals

Mike Unwin

Heinemann Library
Chicago, Illinois

Customer Service 888-454-2279
Visit our website at www.heinemannlibrary.com

Editing, Design, Photo Research, and Production by Heinemann Library
Illustrations by David Woodroffe

Originated by Dot Gradations Ltd
Printed in China by Wing King Tong

07 06 05 04 03
10 9 8 7 6 5 4 3 2 1

Library of Congress Cataloging-in-Publication Data
Unwin, Mike.
    The life cycle of mammals / Mike Unwin.
        p. cm. -- (From egg to adult)
    Summary: Discusses how mammals differ from other animals, their physical characteristics, how they are born and develop, how they reproduce, and their typical life expectancy.
    Includes bibliographical references (p.   ).
    ISBN 1-4034-0782-7 (HC) 1-4034-3407-7 (PB)
    1. Mammals--Life cycles--Juvenile literature.   [1. Mammals.]
    I. Title. II. Series.
    QL706.2.U69 2003
    599--dc21

                                    2002011710

Acknowledgments
The Publishers would like to thank the following for permission to reproduce photographs:
p. 4 FLPA/Sunset; p. 5 Ardea/M. Watson; p. 6 NHPA/ Ann & Steve Toon; p. 7 Bruce Coleman/William S. Paton; p. 8 Ardea/Augusto Leandro Stanzani; p. 9 Oxford Scientific Films/Liz Bomford; pp. 10 (top), 19, 21, 24 (bottom) Corbis; p. 10 (bottom) NHPA/Martin Wendler; pp. 11, 13 Nature Picture Library; p. 12 FLPA/R. P. Lawrence; p. 14 Ardea/Jean-Paul Ferrero; p. 15 Oxford Scientific Films/Mark Deeble & Victoria Stone; p. 16 FLPA/Minden Pictures; p. 17 Ardea/Chris Brunskill; p. 18 NHPA/Laurie Campbell; p. 20 Ardea/Francois Gohier; p. 22 Oxford Scientific Films/ABPL Photo Library; p. 23 Oxford Scientific Films/Ben Osborne; pp. 24 (top), 26 Getty Images; p. 25 FLPA/Jurgen & Christine Sohns; p. 27 FLPA/ Minden Pictures.

Cover photograph of the new-born elephant, reproduced with permission of Oxford Scientific Films.

The mammal at the top of each page is a gorilla.

Every effort has been made to contact copyright holders of any material reproduced in this book. Any omissions will be rectified in subsequent printings if notice is given to the Publishers.

Some words are shown in bold, **like this.** You can find out what they mean by looking in the glossary.

Contents

Look but don't touch: Many mammals are easily hurt, and some may bite or kick. If you see one in the wild, do not get too close to it. Look at it, but do not try to touch it!

What Is a Mammal?

All mammals have a backbone and so are known as **vertebrates.** Their bodies are supported by skeletons of bone called **endoskeletons,** and they breathe air with their **lungs.** Mammals are also **endothermic,** which means that their bodies turn food into energy to keep them warm. Mammals feed their babies on milk and care for them as they grow up.

A pangolin looks more like a reptile than a mammal. But underneath its hard, shiny scales, it has a soft furry belly, like most other mammals.

All kinds

There are more than 4,600 different **species** of mammals, including mice, cats, horses, and humans. Most are furry or move on four legs, but some are different. Whales are mammals that live in the oceans. Like fish, they have smooth, hairless bodies and fins to help them swim. Bats are flying mammals that catch their food in the air. Like birds, they have wings to help them fly. Human beings walk upright on two legs.

How Are Mammals Born?

A female mammal produces tiny eggs. She does not lay them, like birds do. Instead, they are **fertilized** inside her body by the male's **sperm.** A fertilized egg develops into an unborn baby, called a **fetus.** The fetus grows inside the mother. In most mammals, the fetus gets food and **oxygen** through a special organ called a **placenta,** which grows in the mother after she becomes pregnant.

Waiting to be born

A fetus develops and grows inside an organ in the mother's body called a uterus. The time the fetus is in the uterus is called the **gestation period.** The length of a gestation period varies from one mammal to another. In African elephants it lasts nearly two years. In mice, it lasts three or four weeks.

A safe place

Female mammals must find a safe place to give birth. A polar bear digs her den in the snow. A rabbit makes a soft hollow in the ground and lines it with her fur. A gray squirrel makes a nest in a tree.

A polar bear gives birth deep inside her snow den, where it is much warmer than outside.

Some female **social mammals** leave their group to give birth in a secret place. The female fallow deer does this. She introduces her baby to the rest of the herd when it is a few weeks old. Elephant mothers give birth right in the middle of the herd. There, the other members of her family can help her protect the calf from danger.

When an elephant is born, other members of the herd get very excited and crowd around the mother and baby to watch and help.

Headfirst into the world

Most baby mammals are born headfirst. The head of a newborn human baby can bend and squish because the **skull** bones have not yet joined together. This allows its big head to squeeze more easily out of the mother during birth. After a few weeks, the baby's head forms into a more rounded shape.

The spines of newborn hedgehogs are hidden underneath the skin, so they do not hurt the mother during birth. A few hours after they are born, the spines poke out and start to grow.

Hiding the evidence

Once a baby mammal is born, the **placenta** is no longer needed, so it comes out of the mother. A used-up placenta is known as afterbirth. Some female mammals, such as gazelles, bury or even eat their afterbirth. They do this because the smell of the afterbirth can attract **predators** to their babies.

How many babies?

Some mammals, such as rhinos, give birth to just one baby at a time and then wait a few years before having another. Most smaller mammals give birth to **litters,** or groups of babies, and give birth more often. Every year, female hamsters give birth to 2 or 3 litters of about 10 babies each—that's 20 to 30 babies every year!

Born underwater

Unlike most mammals, a baby dolphin is born tail first. This allows it to get oxygen from its mother while it is being delivered underwater. As soon as the baby is born, the mother nudges it toward the surface to take its first breath.

A newborn dolphin weighs up to 45 pounds (20 kilograms), which is about one tenth of its mother's weight.

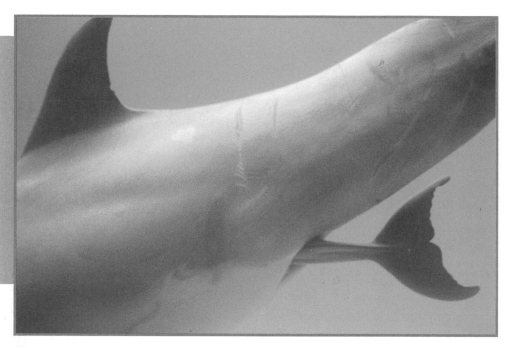

Population explosions

When there is plenty of food, female Norwegian lemmings have a **litter** of five to eight babies. After only four weeks, these babies can have litters of their own. The number of lemmings increases very quickly. This is called a population explosion. However, with many new mouths to feed, the food is quickly eaten up. Many lemmings die, and **breeding** slows down among those that remain.

What Do Baby Mammals Look Like?

Many newborn mammals, including cats, mice, and rabbits, are completely helpless. They do not look much like their parents. They have little or no fur, and they cannot walk or even see. Human babies are among the most helpless of all. They cannot even sit up until they are at least six months old.

Newborn gray squirrels are naked, blind, and toothless. Fur starts to appear after two weeks, and they first open their eyes after one month.

Ready to go

Some newborns, such as giraffes, look just like their parents—only much smaller. They are furry and can see clearly at birth. This is because these animals are **prey,** or animals that are eaten by other animals, and they live in the open. At first they are a little wobbly, but within minutes they can walk and very soon they can run. This helps them to keep up with their mother and escape from lions and other **predators.**

9

A mother giraffe uses her long tongue to clean her newborn baby.

Keeping out of trouble

Some mammals are born with patterns that disappear as they grow older. These patterns serve as **camouflage** that helps them blend into their surroundings. A baby tapir has spots and stripes that look just like the pattern of light and shadow on the **tropical rain forest** floor where it lives. When she goes to search for food, a female tapir knows that her baby is well hidden from predators.

It is hard for predators such as jaguars to spot a baby tapir because of its markings, which serve as camouflage.

Who Takes Care of Baby Mammals?

Because newborn mammals cannot take care of themselves, they stay close to their mothers all the time. A kangaroo stays inside its mother's **pouch,** a baby anteater rides on its mother's back, and a baby bat takes shelter beneath its mother's wing.

Baby shrews attach themselves to their mother in a chain. Each baby uses its sharp teeth to hold on to the one in front of it. This is called caravanning. If the babies can't find their mother, they attach themselves to the first moving object they see.

Dangerous strangers

Sometimes female mammals have to protect their babies from an adult male of their own **species.** Female lions often have to do this. The dangerous male is not usually the father. He is a stranger from outside the group who wants to mate with the female. He will even kill her babies to do so.

Nursing

In addition to protecting their babies, female mammals also feed them. Unlike reptiles or birds, all female mammals produce milk. Milk gives babies the nourishment they need to grow. A female fur seal's milk is more than half fat. This helps her baby gain weight quickly. Milk also contains **antibodies,** substances that protect animals from **germs.** The babies get the antibodies when they drink the mother's milk.

Milk is made in the mother's **mammary glands.** Some female mammals, including apes and elephants, have two mammary glands on their chest. Each one has a nipple on the end, which the baby sucks to get milk. This is called **nursing.** Mammals that give birth to larger **litters** have many nipples, or teats, along the underside of their bodies.

A pig has six pairs of teats, so it can nurse up to twelve babies at the same time.

Toothless

Many baby mammals, including humans, are born without teeth. This means they can nurse from their mother without hurting her. Teeth grow when the babies are ready to start eating solid food that needs chewing.

Bringing up baby

The mother takes care of most baby mammals. A male tiger disappears long before his cubs are born and will probably never meet them. Some parents, such as South American titi monkeys, stay together to share the work of raising their babies. Among certain **social mammals,** including elephants and dolphins, the youngsters also play an important role in caring for the babies in the group.

Young black-backed jackals help their parents out by feeding and caring for the pups.

Why does a kangaroo have a pouch?

Marsupials are mammals with **pouches,** such as kangaroos and koalas. Unlike other mammals, a female marsupial does not have a **placenta** to feed her baby while it is developing. This means that marsupials have shorter **gestation periods** than most other mammals. Their babies are born early, so they can start **nursing** as soon as possible.

A baby kangaroo is born after a gestation period of only one month. It is blind, pink, and only about 2 inches (5 centimeters) long—about the size of your thumb. Luckily, it has a good sense of smell and strong little front legs to help it climb up to the mother's pouch. There it latches onto her teat to nurse. It stays inside the pouch for more than six months.

Egg-laying mammals

Monotremes are the only mammals that lay their eggs. Like most marsupials, they live in **Australasia.** There are two kinds of monotremes—the duckbilled platypus and the echidna. A female duckbilled platypus lays two eggs, which hatch after about ten days. Like other mammals, the babies feed on milk from their mother. Because she has no teats, her babies suck the milk from the fur around the openings of her mammary glands.

How Do Mammals Grow Up?

Baby mammals grow at different rates. A gorilla, like a human baby, grows up very slowly, and only starts to walk after seven to nine months. Before then, its mother carries it everywhere, and it continues to nurse from her for three years. Most small mammals grow up much faster. A common vole is ready to leave the nest and take care of itself after only three weeks. After five to six weeks it can have babies of its own.

No more milk

When its mother stops producing milk, a baby mammal is ready to eat solid food. This process of change, from nursing to eating solid food, is called weaning. Once a baby is weaned, it must learn to find food for itself.

African wild dogs make sure that all their pups get something to eat.

From milk to meat

Some parents help to wean their youngsters. When their pups are four or five weeks old, African wild dogs feed them meat that has already been chewed and swallowed to make it softer. The meat is then brought back up, called regurgitation. By ten weeks the pups are fully weaned. At fourteen to sixteen weeks, they join their parents on hunting trips. By watching the adults and doing what they do, the pups soon learn how to hunt for themselves.

Learning through play

Playing looks like fun, but it also teaches young mammals important skills. Young male elephants enjoy shoving and chasing one another. This helps to prepare them for more serious fights when they are grown up. Young females prefer running through tall grass and chasing imaginary enemies. This helps them learn how to escape from danger and protect their babies when they become mothers themselves.

When a lion cub chases its mother's tail, it is learning hunting skills that will help it to survive in adulthood.

How Do Mammals Find a Home?

Mammals need a place to live that provides them with food and safety. Some mammals, such as dormice, spend most of their lives in one small area. Others have a large home **territory.** For a pack of arctic wolves, this area can cover more than 15,400 square miles (40,000 square kilometers).

Moving out

Many young mammals have to find a place of their own when they grow up. After about sixteen months, a tiger cub leaves its mother and moves away. The mother usually will not spend any more time with her grown-up cubs so that she can concentrate on raising her next **litter.**

Once a young adult tiger has found a place of its own, it usually will not try to return to its mother.

Leaving the herd

Most male and female mammals grow up differently from each other. Young female impalas stay with the herd they were born into and have their babies. Young males are driven out by the **dominant** male as soon as they are grown up. These outcast young males form small **bachelor herds** of their own. In time, each one will try to join up with a new group of females.

Building a home

Some mammals build a permanent home where they spend their whole life. European badgers dig a system of tunnels

known as a sett. One sett may be used for hundreds of years by many generations of badgers. Other mammals make temporary shelters. Every night an orangutan builds a new nest of branches up in a tree. This means it can always stay near a new food supply.

A European badger sett may have more than 100 entrances and exits.

Rodent construction workers

North American beavers live in small family units. They use their strong teeth to chew through small trees and branches, which they pile up to make a dam across the river. This slows the river down to create a calm pond. The beavers then use more branches to build their home, called a lodge. There they can bring up their young in safety.

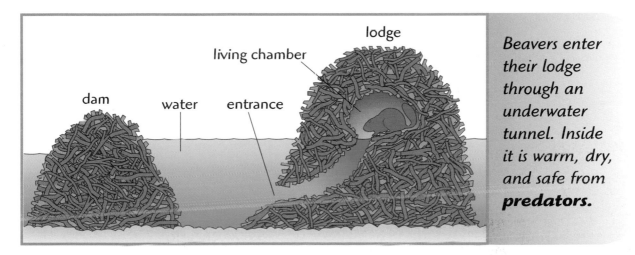

dam water entrance living chamber lodge

Beavers enter their lodge through an underwater tunnel. Inside it is warm, dry, and safe from **predators.**

Following food

Some mammals have to **migrate** to find food. In eastern Africa during the rainy season, wildebeest gather where there is plenty of grass to eat. When the rainy season is over and the grass is gone, the wildebeest migrate to new feeding grounds. When the rains return, the animals migrate back to their original feeding area, where the grass has grown back.

Blue wildebeest have to face many dangers during migration, such as fast-flowing rivers full of crocodiles.

Whale of a journey

A gray whale spends the summer in the Arctic Ocean, feeding from June to October on plankton and other tiny sea creatures. In the winter, when the ocean freezes, it migrates south down the west coast of North America toward the warm waters of the **equator.** There, during February, its baby, or calf, is born. The calf nurses on its mother's milk to grow strong enough for the long journey north again in summer.

PACIFIC OCEAN

Migration route

CANADA

UNITED STATES

MEXICO

Summer feeding grounds

Feeding grounds during migration

Winter breeding grounds

The 5,600-mile (9,000-kilometer) migration route of the gray whale takes it along the west coast of North America.

A gray whale calf migrates with its mother every year. By the time it is grown up, at twelve years old, it may already have traveled more than 62,000 miles (100,000 kilometers). That is the same as swimming two and a half times around Earth.

Getting along together

Living in groups provides safety in numbers for **social mammals.** Each member of a group has its own position. Usually one or two senior animals are in charge. In some mammals, such as spotted hyenas, the boss is a female. In others, such as chimpanzees, it is a male.

Just like people, chimpanzees use their faces to show each other how they feel.

Moving up in the world

As social mammals grow older, the position of each individual in the group changes. There may be more than 50 baboons in one troop. Each one holds a different position. Once a female baboon has had many babies, she gains more respect from the others. Now younger females will groom her, to make her neat and clean, and help take care of her babies.

When Do Mammals Have Babies?

Once mammals have grown up, they are ready to start **breeding.** This means that males must get together with females to have babies. The **breeding season** is usually in spring, when there is plenty of food available for mothers and babies to stay fit and healthy.

Staking a claim

In the breeding season, a male mammal marks out his breeding **territory.** This lets females know he is there and warns rival males to keep away. Some males use scent. A rhino leaves big smelly piles of dung beside his trails. Others make visible marks. For example, a male leopard scratches a tree trunk with his claws. Still others use sound. The song of a male humpback whale can carry for many miles or kilometers underwater.

A male klipspringer marks his territory. He is wiping a sticky, scented liquid from a gland at the corner of his eye onto a twig.

Bull elephant seals fight fierce battles. Fortunately, their skin and blubber are so thick that they usually do not cause each other serious injuries.

Coming to blows

Males compete with one another for ownership of a territory. Showing off their size or strength is usually enough to avoid a fight. A male walrus with small tusks will not challenge a walrus with big tusks. Sometimes, though, fights do break out. Two male bighorn sheep crash their horns together with mighty blows to see which one is stronger. Fighting giraffes swing their heads like sledgehammers—each one trying to knock the other off balance.

Teaming up

Sometimes young males team up to claim a territory. Two or three young male lions working together can force the older, **dominant** male out of the family group and take his place. Fights between male lions are so vicious that the loser is often badly injured and sometimes even killed.

Mating

Female mammals usually choose to mate with the biggest and strongest males. This means that their babies will probably be big and strong. Weaker males must wait until they are bigger or older before they get to mate. When a female is ready for mating, she is said to be in heat. A male can tell she is ready for mating by her smell. He follows her until she allows him to mate with her.

A pair of mating lions stay close together for a few days.

A male and female porcupine stay together for life to help raise their young.

How many partners?

Some mammals stay with their partners for life. A pair of African porcupines will not separate until one of them dies. They raise many **litters** together, and both parents help raise the babies. The males of other mammals, such as red deer, mate with many different females. This gives them a greater chance of producing healthy babies, but the male does not help raise them.

How Long Do Mammals Live?

The length of a mammal's life depends upon what kind of life it lives. Most mammals never reach old age in the wild. They die as soon as they can no longer find food or avoid **predators.** Animals tend to live longer in **captivity.** There they have no enemies, and people provide their food.

Fast life or slow progress?

Many small mammals lead short, energetic lives. A female common shrew lives for only about two years. But in that short time, she may have up to 30 babies. Each day she eats more than her own body weight in food just to stay alive. Unlike shrews, a female orangutan may reach the ripe old age of 50. But she grows up very slowly and will probably have no more than four babies in her lifetime.

Elephants have few natural enemies, which means they can grow very old. Once their teeth are worn down, they can no longer eat, so they eventually die of starvation.

Common shrew	2 years
Brown rat	4 years
Pronghorn antelope	10 years
Koala bear	18 years
Grey seal	30 years
Chimpanzee	45 years
Indian elephant	75 years
Killer whale	100 years

This graph shows the typical life spans of different mammals if they make it to adulthood.

For richer or for poorer

Human beings have among the longest life spans of all mammals. But human life expectancy (how long someone is expected to live) depends upon how much food, water, and health care people have. Today, in most of Europe and the United States, life expectancy is more than 75 years for men and nearly 80 years for women. In many poor parts of Africa, though, life expectancy is less than 40 years.

Most people can expect to reach old age in countries such as the United States or Great Britain, where they receive plenty of food and medical care.

Mammals in danger

Today, many mammals are threatened with **extinction** because of people. Some mammals, such as tigers and rhinos, are hunted to make money. Others, such as orangutans and lemurs, have suffered because the places where they live have been damaged or destroyed. We humans must try harder to care for the world so that these mammals don't disappear forever.

The golden bamboo lemur is one of the rarest mammals in the world. Today, no more than 500 remain in the wild.

The life cycle

No mammal lives forever. Even so, by the time an adult mammal dies, it will have helped bring many babies into the world. Not all the babies live, but some will grow up to have babies of their own. This is the cycle—from birth to adulthood—in which young are born, grow up, and have young themselves. The life cycle ensures the survival of each mammal **species.**

Fact File

What is . . .

• the longest **gestation period** . . .

The African elephant has a gestation period of 22 months, the longest of any animal.

• . . . and the shortest?

The American opossum and the rare water opossum of South America both have the shortest gestation periods—from 12 to 13 days. Both of these animals are **marsupials.**

• the biggest litter?

The common tenrec, a hedgehog-like mammal from Madagascar, can have up to 32 babies in one **litter.**

• the biggest baby?

A newborn blue whale is about 26 feet (8 meters) long and weighs 2 short tons (1.8 metric tons). This makes it the biggest baby in the world.

• the longest living mammal?

Nobody knows how long the oldest mammal has lived. The oldest recorded person was Jeanne Calment of France, who died in 1997 at the age of 122. Some species of whales, including killer whales and blue whales, can also live for more than 100 years.

• the rarest mammal?

The Javan rhinoceros of Indonesia is one of the rarest mammals in the world. Fewer than 100 remain in the wild.

Can male mammals produce milk?

The dayak fruit bat of Borneo is the only species of mammal in which the males can produce milk to nurse the young.

Mammal Classification

Classification is the way scientists group living things together according to features they have in common. Mammals are divided into three main groups according to how they have their young.

1. Placental mammals

These are mammals whose babies develop inside the mother's body and get food and oxygen from her **placenta** until they are born. There are about 4,400 different species of placental mammals. They are divided into several smaller groups, including:

- *Carnivores:* mammals with sharp claws and teeth for hunting and eating meat, such as cats, dogs, bears, and lions.
- *Sea mammals:* mammals that live in the sea, with fins or flippers for swimming, such as whales, dolphins, seals, and sea lions.
- *Primates:* mammals with well-developed hands for climbing and holding things, such as monkeys, apes, lemurs, and humans.
- *Ungulates:* plant-eating mammals with hooves, such as rhinos, horses, camels, cattle, deer, antelope, and pigs. Elephants are also ungulates.
- *Rodents:* small mammals with strong front teeth for gnawing grain and plants. Rats, mice, and squirrels are rodents.
- *Insectivores:* small insect-eating mammals, such as hedgehogs, shrews, and moles.
- *Bats:* winged mammals that feed on fruit or insects.

2. Marsupials

Marsupials are mammals whose young are born very early and then climb up into a pouch on their mother's body, where they grow and develop. There are about 290 species of marsupials, including kangaroos, koalas, wombats, and opossums.

3. Monotremes

Monotremes are mammals that lay eggs. The world's only monotremes are the duckbilled platypus and the echidna.

Glossary

antibody something in the blood that fights germs inside the body

Australasia part of the world that includes Australia, New Zealand, and New Guinea

bachelor herd group of male animals that stay together until they are ready to breed

breeding having babies

breeding season special time of year when a species breeds

camouflage colors or patterns that help an animal blend in with its background

captivity being kept in a zoo or cage, unable to get out

dominant more important or powerful than others

endothermic producing heat inside the body

endoskeleton skeleton of bones inside an animal's body

equator imaginary east-west line around Earth

extinction dying out of an animal or plant species, leaving no more on Earth

fertilize to cause an egg and sperm to join, which begins the development of an embryo

fetus baby mammal developing inside its mother

germs tiny life forms that can get inside a body to cause disease

gestation period time between fertilization and birth, when a baby animal is developing inside the mother's body

litter group of babies born at the same time to one mother

lung inflatable sac inside the body that holds air, allowing an animal to breathe

mammary gland part of a female mammal that produces milk

marsupial mammal with a pouch, such as a kangaroo

migrate/migration to move from one place to another to find food or a good place for breeding

nurse/nursing to drink milk from a mother's nipple

oxygen gas in the air that animals need for breathing

placenta part of a female mammal that passes food and oxygen through the blood to her unborn baby

pouch pocketlike fold of skin on the front of a female marsupial's body

predator animal that hunts or catches other animals for food

prey animals that are hunted or caught for food by predators

skull bones inside the head that protect the brain

social mammals mammals that live together in groups

species group of living things that are similar in many ways and can breed to produce healthy babies

sperm small cells produced by male animals that join with eggs to create new young

territory area that an animal claims as its own for feeding or breeding

tropical rain forest thick forests of tall trees that grow in hot places where it rains almost every day

vertebrate animal with a backbone

More Books to Read

Goldish, Meish. *Beavers and Other Rodents.* Chicago, Illinois: World Book, Inc., 2002.

Harvey, Bev. *Mammals.* Broomall, Mass: Chelsea House Publishers, 2003.

Morris, Pat. *Sea Mammals.* Danbury, Conn: Scholastic Library Publishing, 2003.

Morris, Pat. *World of Animals: Mammals.* Danbury, Conn: Scholastic Library Publishing, 2003.

Walker, Sarah. *Mammals.* New York: Dorling Kindersley Publishing, 2002.

Index